Practical Life Hacks

Padmapriya Mahendarkar

ISBN: 978-1-7370360-2-9 (Paperback)

The information given in this book should not be treated as a substitute for professional medical advice; always consult a medical practitioner. Any use of information in this book is at the reader's discretion and risk. Neither the author nor the publisher can be held responsible for any loss, claim or damage.

Book cover image "Flowers During Golden Hour" by Irina Iriser
Book design created through www.canva.com

First published by Clean Intellect Publishing 2021

This book is dedicated to
Mama
First Administrative Head of Brahma Kumaris

Table of Contents

All of us need some practical life hacks in handling various problems that come in our daily lives. This book of know-hows will help one to find solutions paving the pathway to peace and happiness. Use a journal to answer the reflection questions at the end of each topic.

How to be Free from Negativity

- Do you feel that you are surrounded with negativity?
- Do you feel that the negativity is slowly invading you?
- Do you feel you are at the verge of being influenced by the external environment?
- Do you get disturbed after listening to a friend's gossip?
- Do you feel helpless in saying: "No" to negativity?
- How can you protect yourself from negativity?

See but Don't See:
I can neither change the negativity nor can I stop someone from being negative. But I can always put a lock on my inner being to prevent me absorbing it. With enough awareness and practice, I can protect myself from any sort of negative atmosphere. I can see the weaknesses, mistakes and injustice of people around me. I can see the wickedness and bad intentions of people around me. I can see the damage caused by the vibrations of other people. But what I do with it within is all that matters.

Whatever comes to the frame of my eyes becomes a thought and all thoughts are just information to my inner being. I take control and become a master in not allowing my thoughts to become emotions that could affect my heart. What happens is that any negative I pick up becomes an emotion during my thought processing. The more I think about what negativity I saw, the more negative I feel about it.

Example: Say at work, I see my colleague getting mad but I am no way related to it. I am passing by and I observe this scene in my office (this is thought — information, your eyes are passing information to your mind). I take this information and process it like "Why is this person mad," "Why he/she cannot be calm," "It is not fair to behave that way." So I let all these thoughts run in my mind and eventually I get a feeling of irritation — negativity around me. I feel that my office environment is negative and everyone is fighting with each other creating a negative environment for me.

Imagine this process is happening to you the whole day at your workplace, streets, anywhere you go and finally when you reach your home, there is another drama waiting for you. You will absolutely feel that there is a lot negativity outside and you are stressed out with all that negativity. Yes, there is negativity outside but along with it there is your own negativity within. Inner negativity is all the emotions like frustration, irritation, fear, anxiety, stress, disappointment and ego.

How to See but Don't Look?
Looking is going deeper and processing what you see. Seeing is merely collecting information.

Looking is giving value to what you see and making it as your own.

In terms of negativity, looking is a disaster, thereby just see the negativity and not look. In terms of positivity, look and dive into the depths of the positivity and make it your own. In the above example,

When I observe the anger scene at my workplace,

- I see (with my eyes and a thought comes to the frame of my mind)
- I consciously say to myself: "It's all right," "Stuff happens!" "Let me send some good wishes and peace to them."
- Rather than questioning, judging and creating my own sense of the situation, I just accept and go to the next level of "giving."
- I give (peace and acceptance) for a short time and move on to my script.
- This way I will feel I am protected and negative-proof.

Hear But Don't Listen:

Similarly anything negative I hear about other people, e.g., bad characters and behaviors, all the awful stuff about what should have happened, what is right and what is wrong, I just hear but don't take it to my heart.

- Whatever others say about someone is not first-hand information (because you didn't see it with your eyes and presence). You are hearing only someone's perception of a scene with his or her thoughts, opinions and feelings.
- You also have a higher chance to get easily influenced by the emotions they are feeling.
- Your relationship towards the gossiped person will definitely change after listening to the negativity.

Say you are hearing your daughter's sharing of how her teacher is treating her. You can be highly misguided by your loving feelings for your daughter, blinding you from what actually happened at school. Especially if your daughter is creating a big scene out of it. You will be biased and may take wrong action towards the teacher and the school.

How to Hear but Not Listen:
1. I hear the negative speaker. I am just collecting information.
2. I do not involve myself in the conversation.
3. I just hear but do not endorse them by saying: "Yes that should have happened!" "Yes, your teacher is so bad."
4. When I convey my feelings to them, I am becoming part of that negativity.
5. I do acknowledge his or her negative feelings but do not blindly believe all they say.

Another example: If someone is afraid and sharing their feelings, I do make them feel safe and support them. I do not give them the feeling of avoidance and show my disinterest neither do I become biased and support them blindly. While taking care of my seeing and hearing habits, I can make myself free from negativity that attacks me from outside. Becoming free from negativity that arises from inside is a whole different story.

Reflection:
1. Write one example where you just heard the conversation?
2. Write one example where you truly listened to the other person?

3. Choose a negative situation where you can apply seeing and not looking. Note down the results.
4. Choose a negative situation where you can apply hearing and not listening. Note down the results.

Om shanti (I am peace)

How Not to Get Disturbed

Sometimes you get annoyed and lose your peace of mind over a situation or person. You begin to feel a disturbance in your mind and after analyzing the cause, you get disturbed even further and drop the reasoning process in despair. Some people suppress their disturbances and some react to it. Disturbance starts with a spark of doubt, discomfort and annoyance and eventually becomes a terrific fire. Initially, the disturbance is ignored but gradually one can't avoid reacting to it. Once you feel the disturbance, time and effort is given to figure out the reason and fix it.

Who disturbs you?
Often we find ourselves pointing fingers towards someone or something due to a disturbance.
Example: "I am innocent and look what others do to me." This inner dialogue often run in our minds. When someone is not matching your ideals or opinions you find them as a disturbance and you tend to get disturbed in their presence.
Example: When your colleague keeps on mocking you, you will find that as a disturbance as your colleague is obstructing your efforts to progress or convey your ideas.
One is the feeling of hurt and being attacked. The other is the fear of not moving forward and finding a threat in your pathway. Basically, anyone who stands against you becomes your disturbance.

Noting a Chart of Disturbance:
- Identify what disturbs you.
- Find those scenes and moments.
- Watch your moods.
- Catch your moments of disturbance.

Stop Looking at Others:
I get disturbed because my awareness and focus is outside and usually upon what others are doing. This habit invites all sorts of disturbances automatically as my mind's door is open for all unwanted to get in. When I keep on checking out what others say and do, I have a higher chance to get disturbed.

The more I look at others, the less I look at myself.

It is like when you are looking at something far away, you lose focus on your nearby area.

Reduce Your Expectations:
Each one has their own priorities, opinions and style of working. They may not match with my ideals and standards. If I keep expecting others to think/speak/act like me, then my disturbance is indisputable. By reducing my expectations, I can be more accommodating with everyone. The more accepting and flexible I am, the less disturbed I will be. Instead of disturbance, my relationships will bring me peace and harmony. So, it is not others that disturb me but my expectations do.

Respect others' beliefs:
All of us have deep-rooted beliefs and it is hard to change them. It takes years to change one's beliefs, especially the ones from childhood. Our minds are so conditioned that we consider all that we believe is the truth. I insist that whatever I believe, is the truth. When I am in this attitude then I am not ready to understand the beliefs of others. I want others to follow my belief because my beliefs are the only truth. I justify my beliefs to others and convince them.

I live my life based on my beliefs and principles and I expect others not to create obstacles. Each soul in this world has their own beliefs and I need to learn to respect them. Their beliefs may be absolutely opposite to my beliefs but I still respect, not reject/annoy/condemn it. I get disturbed and cause a disturbance to others when I disrespect their beliefs. Like beliefs, people's principles, opinions, living style and work style differ. I may not resonate with everything but I still am respectful.

Turning Inwards:
If I should not get disturbed then I should be focused. I allow myself to be focused not in a self-centered manner but with a balance of self-awareness and an acknowledgement of others' presence. I look at myself; in other words I am observing my inner world of thoughts, feelings as well as the outer world of my actions, projects and achievements. In this process, my time, focus and energy is saved from any sort of wastage. Even if something might otherwise be disturbing, I will not get disturbed easily as my mind is focused on my inner world.

Example: While reading my favorite column in newspaper, I totally disconnect from the outside world.

Only when I am free, idle and empty, everything catches my attention quickly. It is like dancing to my own inner beat. I enjoy my being and I am centered therefore I am able to harmonize with others. Rather than getting disturbed with the mistakes, weaknesses and emotions of others, I can offer a heart to listen and understand.

Reflection:
1. Describe the behaviors of people that disturb you?
2. Turn inwards for one day and write down the observations of your type of thoughts.
3. Write one belief of others that you accept and respect now (earlier you didn't).

Om shanti (I am peace)

How to Speak

It might look like a funny topic. But honestly has any one really taught us how to talk and communicate with people? Yes, in our childhood, you would have heard like "Don't use bad words," "Don't speak fast," "Tell the truth," "Don't talk back," "Talk with respect." But no one coached us or gave the training to speak without hurting anyone. Good speaking comes under mannerism; no one taught that either.

We might even know intellectually the right way to talk and communicate but probably we couldn't implement it successfully since we lacked the understanding, method and practice.

Way of Speaking – Present situation:
The majority of the human beings speak whatever they think. One doesn't realize what one speaks especially while being emotional. It is said words are like arrows reaching the heart as its target. So when my arrows are harsh and sharp, it hurts the other.
Observe the way you talk in,
- Anger
- Ego
- Attachment
- Fear
- Anxiety

All the words uttered in negative emotion are poisonous arrows which damage the heart of the other person. They are commanding and demanding words rather than requesting words. People talk without humility, respect and love. Words are filled with demands of their heart and impure intentions are visible in their tone. People feel guilty and worried once the speaking finishes.

How to Speak?
"Speak less, slowly and sweetly" is the slogan in the Brahma Kumaris teachings.
Speaking Sweetly:
Sweetness reflects in our words when we pay attention to "I shouldn't hurt anyone" no matter what they speak or do. No matter how much difficulty I receive, I should still not leave my sweetness. No matter how irritated and frustrated I become, I should never let go of my sweet words.

Sweetness is a beautiful virtue that adds fragrance to the words. Any word spoken with sweetness soothes and melts the other one's heart.

How to create sweetness?
- I change my voice tone. I lower my volume.
- I create love and respect for that soul before I speak.
- I allow my heart to feel the love.
- I also understand the value of that soul's feelings and then when I speak, automatically my tone will change.

The other person can feel my sweetness in my voice. Try it out.

Speaking Slowly:

Each one has a different speed when they speak, some speak quite slowly, some very fast and some mellow. But when we get emotional, the speed changes and we tend to speak faster and louder. Psychologically, as the hearts are far apart, in order to cover the distance, we tend to speak louder to the person sitting next to us.

The moment I start speaking loud, the other person can see only my anger and they will shut off listening. Sometimes I do not realize that I am speaking loud as I have lost myself in my emotions. When I am calm and peaceful, naturally I will speak slowly and clearly and there are higher chances for the other person to understand my words and intentions behind my words.

Speaking Less:

Lots of energy is wasted in our talking. Lots of things don't need an explanation but still we tend to explain it for our own self-satisfaction. You might observe some people repeating the same matters again and again because they want to make sure it's done properly and in their mind, they are not fully satisfied. The reason for this on some level is that they lack trust.

Plan and Communicate:

Rather than jumping to conclusions and conversations, pause and take a few moments to reflect a little deeper and then speak. By reacting quickly to situations, I lose control over my choice of words and speech.

Avoid talking when you are emotional:
Prevention is better than cure. It is a thousand times better to take a pause or borrow some time from the other than to respond when you are emotional and reacting immediately. Sorrow is caused by speaking without thinking twice. Let only jewels of goodness and sweetness emerge from my mouth and not stones of rudeness and hurt.

Reflection:
1. Do my words hurt others?
2. How is my tone of voice?
3. Does my speaking change when I am emotional?
4. What change do I observe in myself when I speak less, sweetly and slowly?

Om shanti (I am peace)

How to Tolerate

Tolerance is a great power used by great people like Mahatma Gandhi and Nelson Mandela to achieve whatever they wanted in life. Some people think tolerance is for the weak but on the contrary, only strong minded souls can tolerate. It is easy to shoot words from your mouth or to attack but it takes great control and power to hold a word inside and not to attack.

How to tolerate?
Tolerance is always done with understanding. Most of us tolerate but we do it with force. We have been given instructions just to tolerate without an explanation of how and why.
Example: An employee being silent when his/her boss yells.

The employee is tolerating but does it as he/she has no choice. But if tolerance is used in the right understanding, it acts as a wonderful situation resolver. Tolerance is always used at the moment of handling someone's tension/anger/bad behavior. After the event of anger passes away, in this case, once the boss calms down, the employee can have a conversation with the boss explaining his/her side of the situation. But if the employee tries to explain himself/herself at the heat of the moment, the argument only continues and the situation worsens. Tolerance can be used as a temporary cooler towards an angry person in order to cool down the other person's reactions. We cannot control anyone else's reaction but we can control our responses. By keeping the bigger picture in mind, the employee can use the weapon of tolerance.

Tolerance when done with force breaks hearts and relationships. People explode and break up because they feel that they have tolerated enough. However tolerance used with love and understanding bridges and creates harmony in relationships. The truth is that everyone has to tolerate something or other to a certain degree in order to achieve something or as a part of life.

Example: To heal from a disease, one has to tolerate the bitter taste of the medicine.

Tolerance is one of the most essential powers in human life. Knowing and understanding the reasoning, cause and effect of a person or situation makes tolerance easy.

It is a belief system to think tolerance is suffering and misery.

Tolerance is a beautiful defensive weapon which protects the heart and unleashes our power of love and accommodation.

Like a tree, tolerance always bears fruits.

One who is tolerant gets the best of everything and they rule. In other words they are the master of what they want to feel. Tolerance is cultivated and developed. I need to use tolerance as one of my options in any given situation. In this fast moving world, no one wants to wait/listen/give time.

I need to incorporate tolerance as one of my choices to deal with people and situations. When I grow this attitude of tolerance, I can be peaceful that nothing can push my buttons and no one can give me sorrow. Tolerance is a powerful weapon to tackle emotions like ego, anger and dominance.

Is Tolerance a weakness?

There are questions like,

"If I tolerate, people will walk on me!"

"I will have no voice!"

"I cannot get my work done if I keep on tolerating everything and everyone."

Tolerance needs to be used only at the moment of the expression of a negative emotion or event by the another. But once the moment passes, I need to communicate and use my power to face/handle. Some people just tolerate all their life without taking any action. They blame life or the person who caused misery to them.

Tolerance doesn't mean I kill my power to act.

No, tolerance prevents my being from acting unnecessarily and fighting. It saves my energy. After I tolerate, I go ahead and use my determination and sweetness to approach the situation. I fix up things and take the right action at the right moment. If I do not tolerate and take a right action, it won't work out either because of the wrong timing (the opposite party is in bad mood).

Let me practice "I am a tolerant soul and use my power of tolerance at the right moment and power to face later on."

Reflection:

1. How is my tolerance level on the scale of 1-10?
2. Write the benefits of a situation I have tolerated instead of reacting?
3. Did I communicate my feelings after I have tolerated? Did I feel in control of myself? How did the other person react?
4. Did I explain myself the process of tolerance with understanding and love? Did I tolerate by force?
5. Do I have the habit of suppression (over dosage of tolerance)?

Om shanti (I am peace)

How to Respect

Do I respect someone for their name, position, status, wealth, talent, specialty, appearance, work, material wealth or relationship?

Real respect is to value someone for who they are; not externally but internally. To respect their inner being beyond their appearance and what they do in life. We tend to respect an official, a delegate and a doctor but do we offer the same respect to a cleaner, newspaper deliverer, store keeper? We might smile at them but do we really respect them from inside? We are programmed to give value to the external labels, masks and only to the great tasks but not simple ordinary ones.

Developing True Respect:
When I respect someone, I create a sense of belonging. Respect makes a person feel good and great. It empowers and motivates a person to continue doing things he/she does. The law of respect is that it doesn't come to those who seek it. Respect is earned automatically when I stay in my self-respect. Those who respect themselves earn respect from others.

Respect is a form of appreciation and recognition.

When my attitude is open and equal, I can respect everyone. My vision goes to every being in front of me. I look, recognize and value. We give respect to what we see not what they are. Presentation and appearances draws our attention and respect. They are necessary but quality also matters. Our perceptions have changed and we have become extroverted. **Example:** I might value a seashell hosted in a magnificent showcase; but will I value the same on a seashore?

Therefore I need to look beneath the surface of everything. When I meet a person, I look at the being, their heart, truth, innocence and sincerity. I admire their uniqueness. Sometimes I might not find them in a person, it doesn't mean they are not worthy. I am unable to see it, it is hidden deep within, I just need a magnifying glass. Each one is unique and each role is special and important in their own way.

Respect Vs Good and Bad:
We tend to respect people who do good things and reject or even hate people doing bad. It is said: "Hate the sin not the sinner."

Irrespective of the role a person plays, I respect the person, that is real humanity. Showing respect doesn't mean that I am supporting a person's wrong action but I am just showing humanity which might even bring a small change in the attitude of a person doing wrong. This can be really hard to accept. The reason is we think respect is like a bigger title that can be offered to people who deserve it in our eyes. But every soul in this world deserves a basic respect irrespective of their script.

I cannot offer respect to others because I feel I can teach them a lesson. I take law in my hands and I offer reward(respect) and punishment(disrespect) to people around me based on their behavior.

Respect is Listening:
Respect means listening to one's idea or opinion without judgement. I listen with my full heart not judging or thinking while they are speaking. I make myself available to the present moment and give my attention. Sometimes people don't need anything except a listening ear and your genuine presence.

Listening solves many conflicts and issues. When you sincerely listen to someone, the other person feels the respect, care you have and naturally their heart becomes cooler. People become offended when they are disrespected, ignored/ rejected. Each soul in the world deserves respect irrespective of who they are. When I give respect, I make them belong to me and this belonging draws unity, love and more than anything else, brings transformation.

The Myth of Earning Respect:
We have been taught from childhood that we should earn our respect by getting good grades, graduating from a top school, six figure salary, inventions and awards. Young or old, A grade or D grade, winner or loser, family or stranger, everyone deserves basic respect. Basic respect is valuing that person as

a fellow soul in this world doing his/her unique part in the world. Respect has become like a prize or a medal given to only someone who achieves something. Respect and value has to be given for all accomplishments but it doesn't mean others are not valuable and do not deserve respect.

Respect is Gratitude:
To respect someone's time, relationship, opportunities, love and the good deeds that they have done for us. To be grateful is to be respectful. To take someone for granted, to exploit others and to be insensitive is being disrespectful. To value the time and energy others have invested in us. To respect the invisible sustenance received from people, earth and nature.

Reflection:
1. In my understanding, how much do I respect others and how much respect do I receive?
2. Do I listen? Do I cut off someone while they are speaking? Do I allow others to openly communicate with me?
3. What are my three bullet points to sanction my due respect to someone?

Om shanti (I am peace)

How to be Humble

Humility is a state of mind where one is able to be calm and peaceful even when respect is not given. One is able to give respect and be cool even in the situations of,

- Insult/Defamation
- Blame
- Being put down
- Taunting
- Anger
- Rejection

Usually one tends to react to such situations and being humble seems undermining and impossible. However humility and coolness go hand in hand. Only those who are humble can be cool. An arrogant person easily loses his/her temper and peace of mind whereas a humble person can retain his/her cool mind with a loving heart.

The Humility Drama:

For some people, humility is natural. It might be their specialty or they would have developed it in their childhood. Humility doesn't mean the absence of the power of speech and action. Being humble doesn't mean that you,

- does not take initiative
- show a non-caring attitude
- wear false masks to depict good image
- have to be quiet
- never speak up

- never communicate

Rather humility is connected with greatness — your generosity, big heart, brotherhood and holding an accepting and forgiving attitude. Humility is such a power that doesn't allow you to get hurt with the interaction of others.

Being humble is to observe and not react immediately.
A humble person knows how to respect himself/herself.

Being humble means,
- I do not expect respect from others.
- I do not draw my portrait based on the views or opinions of others.
- I do not wait for acknowledgements and appreciation for my tasks.
- I do not do any task for anyone's sake; I do it for my happiness and for my being because I love helping others/I love finishing my tasks on time/I love arriving on time.

How do I develop humility?

The more I learn and communicate with my own being, the more humble I become. The armor of humility gets created when I develop love and respect for myself. Developing humility is a process because it is connected with how much value I give to what I think/feel about myself in comparison to what others think/feel about me.

When the self-image is clean and clear then I am able to see my specialties and weaknesses clearly; accept them completely with no questions or doubts. I honestly work on my weaknesses and be patient with my transformation. Even when someone criticizes or points out my defects, I can humbly accept their behavior and it won't hurt me because my humility has shown me clearly who I am. There is no need to feel bad because I am aware of my defects and I love myself as I am. This trust and understanding about myself will protect me from hurt. It is not even a big deal when others pinpoint my mistakes.

I do not take comments/hurts/insults personally at all even though it's true. I embrace it, hold my self-respect, take it easy and move on. This is humility. When I am operating in such a humble mind frame, no one can disturb me, no one can push my button and even though they do it, it doesn't bother me anymore. Only when I am not affected, can I smile and behave normally with people who do that to me. Otherwise my face turns red or I get mood-off and I will avoid them. I will continue reacting, blame others for what they did was wrong, try to gain mercy or be a victim.

Now, let me wear my armor of humility and smile towards everything as I know the power within.

Reflection:
1. What is your percentage of humility? Do you consider a humble person to be less powerful?
2. With the help of this book, how will you develop your self-respect?
3. Practice humility for one week and write down the results.

Om shanti (I am peace)

How to be Happy

Happiness is a constant decision I make at every step of my life. Due to my negative thinking, I always find something to feel sad about. My mind is so accustomed to being worried and being sad, that at times when I find everything is going well, a little fear pops up "Ooh...it's odd everything is going well... something is fishy here..."

By drawing attention, I become skeptical about my rhythmic happiness which life is bestowing on me due to my good karma (actions). With this self-criticism, my sub conscious mind automatically invents or hunts for a little tiny loophole in my rhythmic happiness and "Boom" my happiness disappears in a flash of a second.

What happened? Who took it away?
"I"

Rather than enjoying the happy things coming to me, I become overwhelmed, extra cautious, skeptical, critical and build an anonymous fear. I become the sole reason to chase away my incoming happiness.
Example: I doubt the authenticity of a person in front of me, rather than appreciating his/her genuine behavior, I develop doubt and push the person away.

It is subtle and interesting how I influence the energy, atmosphere and events that come to me. Such is my power to create...I am so powerful.

So whenever things move well,

- I accept it.
- I let it flow.
- I don't judge or become anxious.

I naturally respond to events and situations. When things collapse according to time, I hold my inner peace and happiness and treat it from my inner space. I can exercise better control on the situation and inspire people, when I am strong inside — stable, clear, non-dependent.

Illusionary Permanent Happiness:

Right from childhood, the entire world has taught me that happiness is waiting for me outside and I have to go and claim it. Happiness can be found in places, people, materials and the pleasures of the world.

Examples: exotic properties, travel and explorations, luxurious facilities, clothing and jewelry.

The quality of happiness I receive from those is only temporarily fulfillment. Say I spent a weekend in Hawaii, I enjoyed and it was refreshing, but how do I feel on that Monday morning.

- Was the happiness I experienced able to give power for my future?
- Is it able to transform all my sorrow into happiness?
- Was it able to heal me and give a new boost or refreshment?

Realistically No, it did refresh my mind to some extent, and I am back again to the pool of my worries and routine life. It is not that I shouldn't go to Hawaii, I do go but along with my body, I also need to find means to reinstate my soul to true happiness.

Real Happiness:

Real happiness is the one that makes my being powerful. The impact after the attainment of happiness should be strong.

Real happiness transforms tears into pearls, scars into gifts, and sadness into joy. It gives a meaning for all the challenges I underwent, clears the path ahead and helps me enjoy the journey.

Real happiness motivates the self to appreciate everything around you. It provides the sharp lens to note minuscule specialties of people and hidden benefits of situations. Real happiness doesn't rely on how people treat me. Real happiness is like a fountain that constantly flows from within. No dependency — no limits — no bondage — no tags.

How do I create real happiness?

I need to understand my inner power. If I have the power to create sorrow, I also have the power to create happiness. Tap into my inner potential and practice the formula of happiness. I create sorrow because I constantly think about others.

Why do I think about others?

Because I believe, they are holding the keys of my happiness.

My happiness has multiple keys. I have given one key to my spouse, one to my children, one to my boss, one to ......

Why did I give away the key? Who asked me to give it?

The belief system I created since childhood or even before. I believe that keys are supposed to be given to others. No one told me to keep the key with me. I saw everyone giving their keys to others so I did the same. I, in turn hold the keys of others. When I was a child, my mother gave her key of happiness to me. I played with it. As a return, I gave my key to her. As a result, I am stuck with this habit of wanting/claiming/expecting/demanding happiness from outside.

How will I get my key back?

I just have to find the keys, identify them and restore them to their own place. I cannot immediately grab my keys from others; it is a gradual gentle process. I teach myself to change my belief system of happiness.

Whenever any situation or person is using their keys to give me sorrow, I talk to myself: "I hold my happiness key, let me delete this expectation. Let me gradually take my key back from them...they are playing their role... it is my decision to pick up or skip the sorrow given to me..."
I go beyond right and wrong and I understand that they cannot make me peaceful or happy as they themselves don't have the key. So I am the master of my mind, I let it go and create happiness from within.

Reflection:
1. Identify your keys and write the location of your keys.
2. Try to get one key back and note down the shift you observe in that relationship.
3. Write a moment of your real happiness. What is the difference you see between your own temporary happiness and real happiness?

Om shanti (I am peace)

How to be Content

Contentment is a feeling that helps us to experience spring in autumn and use our magnifying glasses to see what valuable treasures life has given us. The attitude of contentment brings a great deal of satisfaction, happiness, peace and love. The energy of contentment is so enriching that it stimulates zeal and enthusiasm. It motivates, inspires and gives the self a new vision. Where the heart is content, the plate of life is full for them. Where there is discontentment, only emptiness is visible in an assorted plate of life.

Contentment is absence of emptiness. Greed comes from emptiness. Greed wants to acquire everything trying to make the soul content. The truth is I can never become content with material things, people and temporary name, fame and achievements. No matter how much I have, still there is always something missing. I miss the experience of my inner being and inner power. The soul becomes content only with the soul's powers, not with bodily powers and pleasures.

- Am I content with myself?
- Am I content with my parents, spouse, kids, relatives, colleagues, public, and government?
- Am I content with the job I do?
- Am I content with the house where I live?
- Am I content with all the material possessions I own?
- Am I content with my body's health?

In deeper vein:
- Am I content with my actions and behavior?
- Am I content with my personality and habits?
- Am I content with my own spiritual progress?

Contentment is a state of mind that ascertains and finds everything positive and appreciative.

Let me develop the perspective of contentment. A heart that appreciates every teeny tiny bit of goodness and positive occurrence of life.

Examples:
- your car approaches the traffic light and it turns green, you just pass without applying your break
- there are no lines in the post office or bank when you go
- you get a note of appreciation from your colleague
- fresh blooming flowers in your garden
- good health
- sweet loving family
- reassuring friends circle
- uplifting work atmosphere
- opportunities you receive
- your daily nutritious meal compared to the poverty in the world
- your security of the house and country compared to the war struck regions
- all the luxury you have enjoyed when compared to the people who still struggle for the basic needs

Any problem can be solved with the power of contentment. Let us see how,

Obstacles in Relationships:

An obstacle occurs when there is negative thinking about a person or a situation. An obstacle is a blockage of energy flow. This reverse negative energy flow in the heart becomes an obstacle for the soul to experience peace and happiness. You cannot love or respect a soul because of that obstacle – an image/perception of the person created in your mind that is blocking you from being loving/respectful/taking it easy/ letting go of that person's behavior. But with the power of contentment, the original energy I create changes; I see the brighter side of me, the person and the problem itself. I see beyond the damage, hurt, right/wrong, behavior. I do have to make an effort to look for the specialty of that person and magnify that sanguine image gradually in my mind in order to melt the obstacle I have created.

This does require practice, time and patience. Until then, let me do my inner effort and do my best to avoid ejecting my emotions out. I may not like something and it's wrong according to my belief system but let me not express it and hurt people. Let me focus on my inner work.

Contentment with Others:

• I understand that they are doing their best according to their best knowledge (not to my best knowledge).
• I understand their situation and appreciate the effort they put in no matter what how small it is.

- I see the moments of our relationship and the time spent together from their angle (where they are coming from).
- I fathom that people are different and so are their capacities and abilities, thereby I do not expect them to meet my measure.
- I concur with the truth that no one is perfect in this world.

Contentment with the Self:
- Do I love, respect and admire myself always?
- Am I content with myself?
- Do I suspect myself? The last person to love me is "me"?
- Do I get annoyed with my own being sometimes?
- Do I hate my weaknesses and feel unworthy?

Similar questions rise and fade in our minds daily as we sail the journey of life undergoing happiness and sorrow. I daily count all my attainments in life. I keep it in my awareness and constantly remind myself. I create a pure beautiful image of my true self which is full of all virtues and powers, completely free from all vices and deception. When I forget the inner beauty and inner treasures I own, then I start seeking these treasures of love, respect, peace, happiness from outside. When I do not get them at my desired quantity at desired time, then I become discontent, disappointed and depleted.

I can stop this cycle by practicing the awareness of my inner beauty and by looking at the self beyond the thoughts, feelings, actions and words. I am not my thought, feeling, action or word rather I am the creator. I need not get bombarded from my creation but as a creator I take responsibility of them. This understanding will keep me content and eradicate my errors and mistakes.

Contentment with Situation/Events:
There are many incidents, events and situations that happen in our lives that are horrible, devastating, frustrating, damaging and depressing. The play is of both happiness and loss, profit and loss, truth and false, praise and defamation, victory and defeat, good and evil. In the good scenes, we easily feel the peace, love and benevolence it delivers us. But in the worst scenes, they are hidden. It is like a gift in an unattractive ugly wrapper. I need to find the heart, courage and hope to remove the wrapping to discover the gift.

Similarly in life, at challenging times I have to use all my resources to keep me going and use the powers of truth, courage, acceptance, enthusiasm, hope, faith, patience, tolerance and perseverance. Like a butterfly emerges from the struggle of the cocoon, I have to undergo the struggle to make me stronger and experienced. Sometimes I literally have to hunt for the benefit in every scene that is hidden. It is not easily visible for our physical eyes and our negative thinking minds. But it is there, I am just not looking for it. Let me work from the space of contentment to generate and spread happiness all around me and create a world of happiness.

Reflection:
1. Write your percentage of contentment of the self, others and situations.
2. Hunt for three hidden benefits from adverse incidents.

3. Why do you think that a certain person will not give you a certificate of contentment? Can you try to claim it?
4. Whom will you give your certificate of contentment and for what reasons?
5. Why you are not content with yourself? Write three reasons and resolve with the above solutions. Jot down the results.

Om Shanti (I am peace)

How to be Grateful

Gratitude,
- Gives me happiness and contentment.
- Makes me appreciate.
- Stops all my complaints.
- Makes me smile.
- Opens new perceptions.
- Allows me to wait patiently.
- Removes all confusions.
- Heals everything in its own way.

Why I should be grateful?
When I am grateful, I live a life of awareness. I acknowledge all the positive and good things in my life and around me. I use my inner eyes to develop the power of gratitude. Gratitude is an ability to see things beyond the surface. A grateful person definitely has a positive attitude, kind generous heart and high self-esteem. My life will be felt full and whole no matter what comes when I see it with the spectacles of gratitude.

How can I be grateful?
Take a moment of silence and go to the space of your heart. Ask yourself,
1. What do I have which some people in the world are deprived of?
Example: healthy body, food, water, house, transport

I am grateful for it ...

2. What are my specialties, strengths that naturally are in me that many souls are trying to practice or just don't have?
Example: honesty, tolerance, forgiveness
I am grateful for it ...

3. What are my gifts and talents?
Example: excellent cook, singer, innovative, forgiveness
I am grateful for it ...

4. What are the lessons that life has taught me so far?
Example:
a. Losing a job has taught me confidence, creativity and determination.
b. The conflict in a relationship has taught me patience.
I am grateful for it ...

5. What transformation this year/last year has brought in me?
Example:
a. In this year I started paying more attention to my health or family.
b. This year made me realize ....
I am grateful for it ...

Gratitude thinking can become a habit and even part of my personality when I pause frequently to thank. I thank myself, God, people, nature, life and everything. Every day I find something to thank for, in order to keep up my spirit of gratitude.

Why I am not grateful?
Taking it for granted:
The sign of not having gratitude is to take people, objects, facilities and the opportunities given to me for granted.
Examples:
- A spoilt kid who do not know the value of $100.
- An adult spending thousands of dollars on expensive shoes.
- A student wasting his/her precious time in unhealthy activities.

When I take things for granted, I hurt the responsible ones who provide/care for me.

I tend to waste their time, energy and resources without realizing the damage I cause. I even take my own life for granted. I do not value my body's health, relationships and resources. I use them carelessly without paying attention. It is said that the value of anything is truly realized only when one loses it. Therefore gratitude frees us from repentance. When I live gratefully, I will never regret rather be content.

Maturity:
I cannot be grateful when I lack maturity. Maturity is the ability to understand and get the sense of everything beyond the selfish needs and motives. Maturity helps one to see the bigger picture and allows one to be calm instead of reacting hastily. Often in childhood, one is taught to be grateful by one's parents, e.g., to pray before the meals. Even though it is

done as a routine, one gets the idea of gratitude. Some do not develop maturity at all.

When I think: "I deserve it":
When I feel I have the right to it, I only demand. As I believe: "I deserve it," I do not feel obligated to be grateful. I reserve gratitude for special things, so why should I be grateful for my right? This attitude doesn't allow me to be grateful.
Example: the share of your grandfather's property
One might feel grateful if one receives something after making a lot of effort. The fruit of the effort ignites their feeling of happiness and gratitude.

Gratitude has an expiration date as well:
We all expect someone to be grateful. Say we did a favor or help someone, we expect that person to favor back at least in need. According to the Law of Karma, all accounts of give and take among human beings is 1:1. We expect 1:10, we do one action and we want 10 actions returned from them in the name of gratitude. If someone gives you more return say 1:5, then it's just their kindness, generosity and good karma, I.e., not to take it as they are returning your good deed and keep expecting it more and more.

Only God can offer one:multimillion times return of your pure actions towards goodness and divinity. Check do I expect someone to be eternally grateful to me?

Reflection:
1. Make a list of 10 things you are grateful for.

2. List 3 things for which you are not grateful but should be? Why you are unable to be grateful?
3. Do you feel that someone is ungrateful? Can you verify if it is your expectation or reality?
4. Rate your percentage of maturity. In what aspects do you still need maturity?

Om shanti (I am peace)

How to Manage Time?

Time is an invaluable treasure. Time is impartial. Time is common for all the souls of the world. Time waits for no one. Time never betrays. One can always count on Time.

Time and Actions:
Actions performed at the right time have value. If the time is missed or the same action done at the wrong time it leads to different effect.

Example: While baking a cake, the cake has to be pulled out at a certain time, if that time is missed the cake doesn't turn our right.

The accuracy of time has its own benefits. The world moves on a certain timeline. The way I spend my time defines my uniqueness in this world. One becomes Mahatma Gandhi with his time and one becomes Adolf Hitler with his time. The quality and timing of actions decides one's destiny. To help someone in need is the biggest charity and yields more good score than to donate something you have extra to someone. The accumulation of positive and negative karmic accounts (The Law of Karma/Actions) works on the accuracy of the time the deed was performed.

Example: If I refuse to help someone who is desperate, it accumulates more negative points. The intensity of the necessity of the person at that moment is taken into account by the Law of Karma.

And not every action's consequence is reaped immediately. In terms of Karmic Philosophy, the Time is not linear but is cyclic. So what goes around comes around in the same proportion.

Past, Present and Future:
To live in the present is the best usage of time. If I think a lot about the past and worry about the future, I only waste my current precious time. I need to value and utilize the beautiful moments available for me today. The freedom and choice I have to use my time is a privilege. Not everyone gets this privilege to use their time as they like.

Is there a good time or bad time?
There is no good time or bad time. It is just my perception.
Perception of Time:
The way we perceive time is based on my,
- mood and emotions
- personality
- belief system

If I am in a happy mood, when guests knock my door bell, I am excited to have them but if I am in a dull mood, I do not enjoy anyone's company. If I have an enthusiastic personality, even when mishaps happen I handle them in a positive manner. I will not complain that this is a bad time or blame my fate. My belief system plays an important part in perceiving Time. My culture, childhood beliefs influence how I see occurrences in life.

Example: People who believe in astrology perceive time and events in that view point.

How to Manage Time:
- Conquer laziness and carelessness.
- Be determined.
- Keep an aim and objective in your life.
- Work towards short term goals.
- Appreciate your progress.
- Be sincere and hardworking.
- Find out where your time gets wasted.
- Plan your day efficiently.
- Prioritize important and minor tasks.
- Check your progress daily.
- Create balance between family and work.

To manage time is an art that can be easily picked up by everyone who want to learn. I need to be determined to achieve something in my life in order to use my time efficiently. If I have no goal, then I will be careless and lazy to even appreciate things I have. I will be mindless in wasting not only my time but also the time of others.

Managing time doesn't mean that I need to account for every second of my life, that would be a total control freak attitude. I need to be accurate whenever it is needed and I need to completely let go of time-consciousness at certain situations.

Example: Say I am on a vacation with my family. I need not be time conscious to wake up on time and do everything on time. Here, I just follow my heart and allow my feelings to guide the time. If I feel like just sitting on the beach, I do that. Then that time becomes my beautiful memory. I don't have to rush my thoughts or plan anything; and not even look at my watch. To completely let go of the awareness of time creates a wonderful time.

Time and Memories:
A time becomes a memory when an emotion is filled in it. We say a bad memory or great memory based on how the time was experienced by the self. To create great memories is in my hands. If I could see the benefit of every situation and enjoy every moment, I am creating a beautiful life. To add a positive flavor at every moment and to see the goodness in every soul is the art of creating wonderful memories.

Always Arrive Early not Late:
It is a good habit to arrive early which will keep the self confident and prepared. When I plan to be early, I allow room for mistakes and mishaps that are beyond my control. Then I will still be on time. I will be free from excuses, apologies and guilt. Use the early minutes for a little pep talk with yourselves, a little prayer or a peaceful moment for the body. When I rush, my heart rate also increases and the body also undergoes unnecessary stress and anxiety.

Benefits of using Time Efficiently:
- There will be no regrets.
- Achieve Success.
- Feel Self-satisfaction.
- Respected by others.
- All my creativity and talents will be well utilized.
- There will be no wastage.
- There will be happiness in relationships.

Reflection:

1. Write an action that you did at the right time like it was the perfect timing.
2. How is your time management? Where do you need help in managing your time? Apply the solutions discussed in this topic and journal the results.
3. Create a time & action plan to achieve your short term goal.

Om shanti (I am peace)

How to Forgive?

Everyone finds it hard to forgive. Most of them are able to forgive little mistakes but find it difficult to forgive big ones. Some hold on to even minor incidents and suffer as they cannot forgive.

Why should I forgive someone?
So that I could be light, free and happy and not hold any grudges inside me. My heart will be cool and healthy. If I hold onto something that keeps on pricking me, I am the first person to suffer.

How can I forgive?
When I let go of,
- blaming the person for my loss/misery
- the person's identity/image I have created in my mind (he/she should behave like this or in a certain way)
- judgement of the mistakes they have made, it may be their:
  — behavior
  — action or words they spoke
  — facial reactions they have given

Also to understand the following,
1. Each one is playing their script. Good or bad, everyone has to play a part in this world.
2. To embrace that I cannot control/change others' script no matter how harmful they are.

3. To see the bigger picture of the damage caused to you by the other.
4. To realize that I am only hurting myself if I cannot forgive. Why should I pay the price for someone else's mistakes?
5. To trust that the Universal Law of Karma will prevail and everyone has to face the consequences of their wrong actions. No one can escape the Law of Karma.

I have recorded the fault of others very deeply in my subconscious mind by repeatedly thinking about it. This is the reason I cannot easily let go of them because each time this past recording is triggered by a present action, it brings the same emotional pain it had caused me in the past. I store and hold onto events that occurred many years ago like childhood experiences. I am stuck with them as they are unfathomably rooted in our hearts.

How to forget?
1. Therefore along with forgiving, I also need to forget — that is the ability to erase the memory (images, words, action, loss, pain) associated with that pain. I can do it because if I can create my memories being a master creator, then I also have the power to delete the entire negative and waste memories I have created by becoming a master destroyer.
Example:
I can forgive someone only when I temporarily remove them completely from their role and relationship with me. Say my spouse did something that hurt me, I can forgive him/her only when I remove my identity/recognition of him/her from the role "spouse" he/she is playing. I should temporarily

disconnect him/her from that role of "spouse" and see him/her as a human being who is subject to mistakes/errors/bad moods/faults.

I bring myself into this understanding that my spouse is not perfect and might have misunderstood me or was just not in a right state of mind. I take a positive light of whatever happened. I need not judge a person based on their behavior/action/words. I might have missed their good intention of where they are coming from.

2. When I make the effort to create a record of their positivity and good actions then I can forget. A positive image can replace a negative image in due time. Images exist in the mind and my thoughts and feelings create those images. With the help of acceptance, good wishes and a big heart, I can notice the goodness of the person who harmed me.
Why should I do this?
If I don't do this, then the negative image I have created about this person, e.g., "He/She betrayed me. It was a horrible experience," the feeling of hatred, misery, resentment will keep haunting me forever. Whenever I see them or hear about them, I will be infuriated. This reaction is not healthy for my body either.

3. Past is Past. To keep past as past and take a lesson from it is a wise choice. We allow past to linger on our minds to such extent that we forget to live the present. Grudges, bitterness and past negative memories will only steal our current opportunity to experience peace, love and contentment. Let

me learn the lessons from my past bitter memories and be careful in my future.

4. Lastly, if I think I do not have the power to forgive, I can connect to the Source, God, the Ocean of Forgiveness to help me forgive. I can transfer my baggage of hurt to Him so that my healing can begin.

The above methods will help me to forgive and forget things like side scenes and move on with absolute lightness and easiness. I live as a cool and free soul.

Reflection:
1. What lessons did you learn from your past bitter memories?
2. Write five positive qualities and actions about the person who you want to forgive. Apply the five points of forgiveness discussed in this session.
3. Write your experience of an incident where you forgave someone. Why did you forgive?

Om shanti (I am peace)

How to be Free from Worry

Why do I worry?

Because,

- I am afraid that something bad would happen.
- I might lose someone/something.
- I would suffer

The root cause of worry is fear, insecurity and uncertainty. There are some more reasons which are discussed below.

Fear:

I worry because I have fear that I might lose my loved ones. I am over-protective of my kids because I fear that something bad might happen to them if I don't worry.

Example: A mother feels worrying is like her duty. If she doesn't worry she considers herself as a bad mother.

Insecurity:

I am insecure, that's why I worry, "What will happen to me if they leave?" "How will I manage?" "This person is so smart, what will I do if he/she takes my position?" "Everyone likes her; what about me?". The above questions are signs of insecurity. When I am afraid that someone will snatch away what I have or when someone becomes a threat for my joy, then I worry.

Imagination:
Worry makes me to imagine all the worst possibilities that will happen in a situation. I create a huge image in my mind and I start to worry looking at that image. As I focus on my inner fear of this image, the outer occurrences get blurred. I lose my discernment of the actual happening of the situation as I live in my own world of worry.

Difference between Worry and Concern & Care:
To have care and concern over loved ones is different from worry. To check on them is caring but to constantly bug them is sign of fear and worry. When I am attached then I start to worry. My peace of mind is dependent on my child's safety. It is fair but to exercise control over every minute of your child is attachment or even obsessive behavior. Worry only puts me in panic mode and I am always restless over something I cannot control. I cannot live my child's life. I need to understand that one in this world is an individual and no matter how much I worry, I cannot steer their journey.

How to be Free from Worry:
Faith and Trust:
Trust plays an important role in not worrying. If I trust and have faith, then I will not worry. Faith and Trust are two powerful virtues that eradicate all doubt and worry. Let me cultivate faith upon the,
• Self
• Source/God
• Others
• Life

Be Open:
I prepare myself for possible occurrences. I have learned from my experience that whatever I have feared the most did not happen ever. And I realize it was just false thinking or waste thoughts that was scaring me like a paper tiger. I blow up my concern into worry, i.e., I make it bigger by thinking too much about it. I have to plan and schedule but as I plan, I prepare my mind to have an open space for the unexpected. This will help me to develop the power to accommodate them when they show up.

Example: I worry I am going to lose my job. I prepare my mind so that even if I lose it, I can always find another job. I build my self-confidence and prepare for the worst. This way even if the worst happens, I will not worry as I am mentally prepared to face the situation.

This sort of preparation will relieve me from unnecessary worries. I am open to enjoy whatever life is providing me at that very moment. When I foresee and plan, I will not worry but if I have expectations that, "Everything should be perfect!" then I will worry whenever things don't go my way.

Power to Face:
If I have the courage and determination to face everything in my life then there is nothing to worry about. If I am unable to face and wonder how will I handle it, then I will worry.

Example: Just like in military, you are trained to face all adverse situations.

Similarly, in life too when we are mentally trained, "Come what may, I can figure out things." This attitude will help me to tread life.

Send a Protective Umbrella:

A visual: As a mother, send a light umbrella of your love, good wishes and protection to your son/daughter. Let it subtly protect your loved ones wherever they go.

Worry Baggage Transfer:

Imagine worry to be baggage. The more I worry, the more my baggage increases. I will feel heavy, frustrated, clueless and confused. Then I will raise a flag of help/support/cooperation and run to my friends and relatives. If I get turned away, I get disappointed and my worry will change into anger, blame and sadness. One of the best baggage transfers is with the Source, God, where I won't get turned away and the actual work is done.

A gentle soothing warming light (Source/God) opens up his arms to transfer my worry baggage to Him and in return, he gives me happiness, intoxication and contentment. When I tell my heart to leave my baggage in his court to sort it out, I immediately feel lightness and contentment. Say you have been wheeling your 50 pound suitcase all around the airport and finally you drop it in the baggage line, recall the lightness you feel. Mental heaviness or burden can be given to God by creating thoughts that,

- God is my companion; it is not just my problem; my companion is present and will take care of it.
- Let my Godly companion figure out things for me; I will relax and allow things to work.
- Nothing is mine; everything belongs to God. I am only a trustee of my body, house, car, children, business, job...

I build a relationship with God with my true heart. He is always on the lookout for me. His help is available 24 hours. His arms are open to embrace and dissolve all my problems in His unconditional love and protection.

I am a carefree emperor who is completely free from worry and always happy, content and intoxicated with what I have in my life.

Reflection:
1. List your topmost three worries at this point of your life.
2. Apply one of the above solutions and write the results.
3. Practice a "Carefree Day" and jot down the observation.

Om Shanti (I am peace)

How to be Free from Stress

Most of us back in our childhood days didn't see life as stressful. But now in the recent times, the famous word that comes from everyone's mouth is "stress." Even a kid says that he/she is stressed. Our lifestyle, goals and work-life have changed. Work has lost its ethics, religion has lost its integrity, and families have lost their tolerance level. If we pay a little attention, we can perform our duties in a peaceful way.

We all fulfill our responsibilities and run our errands but how do we do it?

Examples: All the below actions are filled with stress.
- The way we drive.
- The way we speak.
- The way we take care of others.

We take care of family but we do it with stress, expectations and anger. We deal with work with tension, competition, and blame. We speak with arrogance, rudeness and ego.

Effects of Stress:
When we are stressed, all our actions are shaded with the effects of stress like,
- anxiety
- tension
- bully
- blame
- rude

- frustration
- avoidance

Triggers of stress:

Each of us will have different triggers of stress. Some of the common triggers are:
- when things don't go your way
- when you have a deadline
- while you juggle between multiple tasks
- when someone gives you a hard time
- when your finances are not well
- when there is a loss

Types of Stress and their Remedies:
- Physical Stress
- Mental Stress
- Emotional Stress
- Spiritual Stress

Physical Stress:

Physical stress is very much connected with the body and it happens,
- whenever the body is physically exhausted and under fatigue
- intense traveling
- hunger and lack of nutrition
- illness and disease
- odd working hours like graveyard shift
- lack of enough sleep

All the above physical stress can be managed by paying attention to the needs of the body and by not pushing the limitations of the body. A healthy relationship has to be created between the soul and the body which begins by first listening to the body. Often the body is abused due to your desires, e.g., over-eating your favorite dessert or food. The body doesn't need that much food but your mind does. The body is dragged into many indulgences due to the mind.

Remedies to Relieve Physical Stress:
- get good sleep
- respect your body's limits
- eat healthy (no junk)
- exercise regularly
- pamper your body occasionally, e.g., refreshing bath
- take a break
- plan your rest hour/day

Mental Stress:
Mental stress is connected with the intellectual abilities of a person while performing tasks.
- too much planning
- overthinking
- executing the tasks
- time constraints, target goals and deadlines
- managing multiple requests at the same time
- confusion and unable to make a decision

When there is over-thinking about a matter/project/task then naturally stress builds up. Similarly when you are under pressure to make a decision, you are confused and stressed.

When you need to troubleshoot a technical bug at work, you will get stressed if you are unable to debug after much effort. **Example:** sending the kids to school and getting ready to work on a Monday morning. You are trying to complete all the tasks in a time frame of 90 minutes. You are mentally stressed out during that morning hour. One kid couldn't find her socks, your spouse couldn't his/her keys, you are trying to clean up the kitchen or find your office documents. There is tidal wave of activities in the morning hour and one gets stressed out trying to handle them.

Remedies to Relieve Mental Stress:
In the above example, lack of planning and preparation is the reason for the morning stress. If you have arranged everything you need for Monday morning on Sunday evening, your morning would be a breeze. There shall be no tension finding things as they will be already in place. Lots of mental stress can be relieved if you could,

- plan
- prioritize
- organize
- prepare
- choose wisely
- perform one task at a time
- be flexible when plans don't work out

Where there is mental stress, you are unable to make a decision and prone to mistakes. When you sufficiently prepare and execute your tasks calmly then the mental stress is averted.

Emotional Stress:

This is the most common stress that happens in relationships. You get emotional stress when there is,

- difference of opinion
- absence of love and respect in a relationship
- arguments and conflict
- jealousy and envy
- ill treatment and discrimination
- lack of acceptance and understanding

Remedies to Relieve Emotional Stress:

- Lower your expectations.
- Adjust and be flexible.
- Tolerate and be patient.
- Listen more and speak less.
- Give more and take less.

Understand each one is unique and doing their best to play their script. Remember "I cannot change/control anyone but myself." When your expectations are not fulfilled, then you get upset and frustrated. Let go of expectations and embrace people as they are including their strengths and weaknesses. Tolerance and patience are powerful qualities that helps one to stay calm and steer the situation in a positive direction. Develop the attitude of giving instead of taking will develop the love and harmony in relationships.

Spiritual Stress:

This stress is related to the identity of oneself. The inner conflict that occurs based on the opinions of others.

Example: You are a kind person but one person accuses you of being a mean person.

Then there is a spiritual stress that occurs within you. You try to prove yourself that you are not a mean person but a kind person. Another situation is when you are being gossiped by others, there is a spiritual stress to clear your image and actions.

Remedies to Relieve Spiritual Stress:
- Believe in yourself.
- Spend time in reflection and contemplation.
- Meditate daily.
- Be kind and compassionate to yourself.
- Do not self-criticize or self-doubt.

With the help of meditation and by paying attention to the self, spiritual stress does not occur. When you know and understand yourself in a clear manner, there are no doubts or the tendency to prove yourself to others. You will be content and confident with yourself. As there is no habit of self-criticizing and self-doubt, there is high self-esteem and an ability to face insults, defamation and accusations.

Way of Peace:
We have to understand that our true nature is peace, I am a peaceful soul and everyone around me is a peaceful soul. Peace is a vibration that the soul emits at its true state. Love, happiness and joy are also the vibrations of the soul. We, souls emit different vibrations at different situations. Anger, attachment, ego are disturbances of these pure vibrations.

This is why we do not enjoy them and dislike them when emitted by us or others.

We can communicate peacefully with love, respect and sweetness. We can also carry out all our routine with calmness, peace and focus. We can take care of others with respect, understanding and compassion. I just have to set my goal that I have to be in peace today and tune my vibration to peace. With peace comes patience, perseverance, tolerance, courage and clarity. I have to remind myself constantly "I am an embodiment of peace," " I am a messenger of peace," "I am a star of peace." Let me enjoy the fruit of doing things peacefully. I will be in much control of myself and the situation.

I will become powerful since I am not emitting negative vibrations anymore. I will be a peacemaker, making others peaceful. My home and environment will become a temple of peace.

Reflection:
1. Write an example of mental stress and emotional stress you have experienced in your life.
2. Write your plan to relieve your mental stress on a Monday morning. Note down the results.
3. Choose a relationship where you experience emotional stress. Apply one of the remedies and jot down the results.

Om Shanti (I am peace)

How to be Free from Judgements

We often come into this crossroad of right or wrong in our lives. Things seem to be right but after few scrolling of life's pages it turns out to be wrong. Parents, Teachers, Scholars and many other sources teach us what is right and what is wrong. But from our own experiences in life, we understand that there is only one absolute truth even beyond the right and wrong dimensions.

There are two angles of right and wrong.
Person's Perception Law:
Something right in one's view is completely wrong in another. Right and wrong is defined by one's land, culture, race, religion, gender and personal beliefs.
Example:
- In the East, white clothing is worn at a funeral and black is non-acceptable whereas at the West, black is worn at a funeral and white is non-acceptable.
- A South Indian person prefers to eat his/her food using hands (as part of their tradition and culture) and it can be belittled by other cultures.

The concept of right and wrong is used as a measure of one's good character. Often in conflicts, one verifies with the another "Did I do the right thing?" When the one gets the acknowledgment that they did right then their mind gets peace otherwise one feels guilty. If people around me label me as wrong, I feel sad and try to prove myself. If they label me as right, then I feel happy. I may even feel proud that I have earned everyone's recognition. The concept of right and wrong is an illusion. I feel my decision is right based on my,

- discernment
- understanding of the situation
- past experiences
- needs and wants
- likes and dislikes
- profitable and beneficial

If the same decision is taken by the other, it will be according to their discernment. Therefore, who am I to judge anyone for their decisions and actions?

Example: A mother desperate to save her child might violate a traffic rule.

I can judge the mother for violating a traffic rule but I fail to see her point of view and the bigger picture. So before we judge, let's try,

- to see other's point of view
- the delicacy of their situation
- their essential needs

To look at the world in only my point of view is discourteous and ungracious. As human beings, it is important to appreciate the differences of each soul that lives in this world.

Universal Laws:

"One needs to observe silence in a library."

"One needs to be polite and humble while making a request."

"Be kind and loving to everyone including animals."
There are common laws that everyone resonate with and unanimously accept them under the right and wrong category. People get angry when the other person breaks these laws.

Emotional Drama:

When people do not follow either the personal or universal laws, I get upset and all the emotional drama begins. I need to understand what I am expecting, is it a personal law or universal law? If I work with people from my egoistic space expecting that things have to be done in my way, then I am making my life stressful and unhappy.

On the basis of feeling of right and wrong, I break relationships. It takes me years of love, time and energy to create one and just one adamant point of "he/she did wrong" breaks it all.

Even if they are not following the universal laws, I need to accept that it is not my duty to govern other's actions and just have good wishes for the person. When I know and accept this truth that I cannot control others' behavior, then I can be a peaceful soul.

Personal responsibility:

I can be careful and alert myself to follow these universal laws of truth,
• Don't give sorrow to anyone.
• Being humble when praised.
• Be polite and honest.

But let me not force my principles on others and react when they don't follow them. Each one is unique and each have their own script to play.

Why do we judge?
To judge hastily is a sign of immaturity and prejudice. When my judgment is biased and opinionated then I will cause hurt to others. To quickly form an opinion about someone is also not a healthy judgment. A judgement is made only after thorough analysis of someone/something. A poor judgment is made by what I see and what I hear about without understanding the whole story. My wrong judgments can cause damage to people around me especially when I am in a responsible position.

The Job of the Intellect:
Right or wrong is decided by the intellect. The intellect discerns and decides. It is said where the heart works, there is no right or wrong.
Example: Your best friend committed a mistake and he/she realizes it and needs your help. In that case, you would keep aside the concept of right or wrong and help her. You use the power of heart rather than the intellect. You will guide him/ her to be truthful and do good.
When I use my heart, I will tend to slow my judgments as my feelings speak louder than my head. In a good judgment, the feelings of one's heart are also considered and not ignored. If it is suppressed then it is a sign of ego. Ego works from the space of the head and not from the heart. When one is egoistic, one's judgements are self-centered and blindsided. A

egoistic person cannot tolerate a difference of opinion and cannot accept that he/she is wrong. So they will fight, argue and blame. They will try to prove themselves to be right and others to be wrong.

Attachment:

I get attached to my notion of right and wrong. I hesitate to accept that I could be wrong because of attachment to my belief system, discernment and judgment. I believe my judgement is always right and I don't make any mistakes. Attachment means being clingy and dependent. When my attached object/person/judgement is opposed or threatened, I become defensive. I cannot easily let go of my attachments as my identities are based on them.

Timing Effect:

Sometimes it is not even about right or wrong but doing right things at the right time. Any task/idea/opinion delivered at the inappropriate moment becomes invalid/wrong.

Example: A wife is excited to share something interesting that happened to her while home, but she shares that with her husband while he just landed at her doorstep. The husband may not give her the right response.

The timing of actions are important, even though it is great, it may turn out to be wrong if delivered at an inappropriate time. The wife can share her heart once her husband has settled down.

Thereby most of our right and wrong arguments are in our minds — our limited thinking and understanding of the people and world around us. When we become open-minded and accept people for who they are and respect their ideas, there are higher chances for people to realize their mistakes and even recover from them.

Reflection:
1. Do you judge quickly? Write 2 incidents where you made a hasty judgement.
2. Does your ego interfere in your perception of right and wrong? Write a situation.
3. Do you get attached to your ideas, opinions and judgements? Write 3 examples.

Om shanti (I am peace)

How to Handle Loss

Loss might be a loss of a loved one, a favorite object, name, fame or anything you treasure. Loss is a feeling of emptiness inside you when you feel something is taken away from you. And the question arises of why it is taken away? What did I do? Was it my mistake? I tried everything but still it is gone? "You don't want them to go but they leave you." This brings you more sadness because you loved him/her but the other person didn't realize or value your love.

You need to remember maybe:
• it is not meant to be
• the other person is not fortunate enough to be with you
• you are saved from future huge conflicts/problems

Love Vs Attachment:
Another reason for your sadness/worry/depression might be that your love got transformed into attachment. Attachment is a web where you lose your identity in the thing you are attached to. You can say you are attached to a person when you emotionally break down completely or feel that it is the end of the world when the attached person leaves you. You can see signs of attachment like possessiveness, getting upset when the attached person is not listening or acting the way you want them to.

Attachment is conditional love that makes you dependent.

Whereas with love, you accept the person the way they are. There are no strings you impose on them directly or indirectly. There is a sense of freedom in love; at the same time there is no hurt. In a loving relationship, either of the people is allowed to live their lives according to their will and there is mutual respect for each other's choices and actions. You love them no matter what. Also when your love is rejected, you still wish them good. True love will not get hurt and will feel hope in life.

The truth is that when someone says: "I love you" they are basically triggering the feeling of love in me. So I am the creator of love. I am love. I can love anyone and everyone. I do not need love from outside nor do I need to claim it from someone. Yes, I can find someone to share my love but there is no dependency in that love. When there is true understanding of love, I will understand the eternal meaning of relationships and I will enjoy life as it comes. I will only give love without any condition or deal.

I am not confining that love to a special one because if I do, it's not love, it's attachment. Then this attachment grows and becomes adamant in programming my mind to receive love only from this attached image/person/object. And I start looking for love only from that direction and when it stops for some reason, I feel lost, empty and betrayed.

Then after my breakup, I start searching for another one again hoping it to be true love, start forming my web of attachment to that person, keep relying on it and when that leaves, and I am back to square one.

In this process, my hearts breaks each time into pieces and finally after many years, I feel I wasn't loved at all nor did I obtain true love ever. The answer is me. I am love. Resonate in this feeling or vibration of "I am love" and observe the magic/ the shift it brings inside you. Then my relationships will last longer, and I will be able to handle all relationships in a much better consciousness.

When a Loved One Passes Away:
"I gave my best care but still the loved one passed away." I talk to myself that I did my best to take care of my loved one. I cannot control the universal laws of birth and death. The loved one left to continue his/her next journey. I send my good wishes which will help my loved one to pass easily. Sometimes I feel guilty that I didn't take good care of them, but it is just a negative thought I create to resist the reality. I cannot stop things. They are out of my control. I give myself the solace and peace that all happens at the right time. I accept it, let go and move forward.

When I am being blamed in such a situation, I stay in my truth and understand that the other person is blaming me because of the sorrow of the lost one, and it is just a projection of their sorrow on me. It is not real and they are unable to handle it on their own. I need to provide support and show maturity in my interactions during those times.

Losing Favorite Objects that are Dear to My Heart:
Things might come and go in life but my happiness shouldn't
go. I should remember that I do not own anything in this
world and nothing belongs to me eternally. Things, materials,
gadgets, jewelry, clothing and all other material objects in the
world do exist for my happiness. The very existence of them is
to make me happy, then why should I lose my happiness when
they disappear? I am the creator, they are my creation.

I always have the power to create something new. Things will
come to me when I deserve and need them. And when they
leave,
- maybe life is teaching me to be independent
- I need to be a master and not a slave to any sort of
  perishable objects
- something new will emerge

I do not design my happiness based on temporary things and
materials. If I am good, honest and clean, my purity will
attract all the happiness in the world without desiring for it.

Losing One's Name/Image:
To lose my image brings the feeling of shame and I am unable
to face others. I feel horrible and ashamed when my
reputation gets debased. I could over-hear their silent gossips
and the subtle judgement of their eyes when I walk by. I have
no way of proving that I am innocent.

Case 1:
I have made some mistakes that spoiled my reputation. But
that is not the end of the world. Mistakes happen. Let me

check to what extent I have realized it and am I willing to change?

If I am sincere, my vibrations of truth and honest efforts will soon change the reputation. People would notice and eventually change their opinion about me. I need not get disheartened and lose hope in such situation. Let me take it as a lesson and move forward.

Case 2:
If I haven't done anything wrong, then I need to understand that images and reputations just exist in people's minds. I cannot take charge of their design. But I need to take care that I do not get hurt and disempower myself with what people think about me. I cannot constantly prove myself to everyone around me. Nothing can take away the truth and yes I need to tolerate the falsehood temporarily but eventually the truth will reveal itself. I need to have faith in myself and life that everything will be all right. The best option at these times is to stay in self-respect and keep myself light and natural. Once people realize the truth, they will even apologize to me and trust me more.

Practice this thought: "I have everything I need at this point of my life. I am content. I believe whatever I need will come to me."

Reflection:
1. What did you lose in life? Write your emotions.

2. Check your attachment levels? Can you change your attachment into pure love?
3. Did you ever lose face? How did you handle it back then? How will you handle it now?

Om Shanti (I am peace)

How to Handle the Games of the Mind

Suddenly a thought arises like self-doubt/a haunting memory/ bizarre temptation/a vague idea that keeps pestering you. These are the games that the mind plays on you, the being.

You are not even sure whether it is really you as you don't create such patterns of thought normally. You don't create them consciously but they just appear in the screen of your mind and you start wondering about them.

Stillness — Be still and let it pass.
Example: When your house doorbell rings, you go and attend the door. Before you attend, you check who is on the other side of the door and you choose to open the door or not. You do not open the door for everyone.
Similarly, I need not process every thought which comes to me. I just have to give it some time, and it will automatically disappear after some time (this might be days or weeks).

I do not question it/analyze/try to understand with my intellect why did it come, what I am going to do and not feel bad about it or confused. If I process them, then I am making a rope into a snake. When you look back on such moments, you will feel wise that you did the right thing by not taking them too personally or seriously. You will discover that they are just passing clouds.

Make Big Matters Small:
When I blow up a small worry or anxiety, I can make it a big obstacle for myself and others. Rather I just give it some time and continue with my routine activities of life and eventually they will finish.

The habit of making smaller things big makes me vulnerable and too cautious about everything that runs in my mind. Sometimes the mind has to be left alone and attention need not be given to every trivial thought in the mind.

If I take everything so personally, then my mind can react as it considers it to be a serious threat to the self. When a situation comes up, let me practice the habit of taking it light and easy. With an easygoing nature, even serious matters will become small stones to cross. When I become nervous, even little matters become big mountains. It all depends on our habits and personality.

Mind and Body:
Often the mind only operates on the present scenario, what I am seeing, what I am hearing, what I am sensing and what environment I am in. Of course the mind does wander off to the past and future, but in an alert state the mind is constantly monitoring the body and seeking inputs from its sense organs — eyes, ears, nose, touch and taste.
It creates thoughts as it constantly senses the environment around to keep one safe. It is the mind's mechanism. The mind can also quickly forget the collected information as it moves on to the next situation the body is in. When anything

deeply affects the mind, that collected information gets an entry pass into the subconscious mind.

Example: You will remember all the details of your wedding day, the dress you wore, how you smelled, how was the environment around you.

Therefore the mind is always collecting and processing the information around us and responds to all the feelings that arise from it. It all depends on one's personality of how they operate their mind and responses.

Example: If I have an introverted personality, even though my mind is observing all my friends and contacts in the party, I may not socialize immediately. The mind will create corresponding thoughts and feelings but the control is in the hands of one's personality and intellect.

Detached Observer:

The best method to tackle any situation is to just watch and observe as a spectator. Just like I watch a baseball game. I am not playing the game but I am watching all the players, the crowd and the game itself. In the same manner, I watch my own being — my thoughts, words and actions. I watch myself speaking to someone. I watch others responding to me.

Reflection: In a tense situation, imagine yourself zooming out of that scene, and watching the whole scene as a third party. What will be your observation? Watch everyone's behavior and reactions.

As I watch, I will notice that I can't control the scene or the players in it. The only person I can control is my own part in the scene.

When I observe, I allow myself to lose the tendency to control others and the situation.

When I watch, I will stop:
• blaming
• disliking the negative behavior of others

The detached observer technique is very helpful in not undergoing the guilt episode about your own reaction to a situation. It prevents haste and unnecessary drama. But it does take quite a bit of practice to master this technique as it is not easy to quickly detach especially when you are involved.

Reflection:
1. What are the games of your mind? Write three.
2. Apply one of the above solutions and write the results.

Om shanti (I am peace)

How to Beat Laziness

What causes laziness?
- routine work
- fatigue/tired
- lack of interest
- boredom
- do not want to put up with someone due to their negativity/ weakness
- no reason — just part of personality

When I am lazy, I don't feel like doing a task or working with a person.

Effects of Laziness:
- procrastination
- avoidance
- inefficient
- you make others wait
- others cannot count on you
- lack of commitment

Lazy with Tasks and Responsibilities:

Example: I am too lazy to clean the garage on a Sunday.
I know it is the right thing to do and it is my duty but I am lazy and do now want to. It is like a dull gloomy weather inside my head. I am cloudy and I want to just hang around.

Excuses:
In order to hide my laziness, I will give excuses and my creativity will shimmer in them. I can create any type of excuse to save my cozy habit of laziness. I may get warnings so I might gear up for few weeks and then I fall back into the same old habit.

Lazy to Deal with Certain People:
Example: I am in no mood to handle someone's tantrum, then I will procrastinate setting up that meeting.
This is a form of laziness too. I am too lazy to put that extra effort and tolerate/adjust with that person. Laziness is like a comfort zone; I am comfortable in my circle of people. I do not want to socialize as I am too lazy to meet new people. Drama will happen and I might get ultimatums in my life due to this habit of laziness. I reform too in some cases. Laziness also causes repentance especially in relationships. I might regret later that I missed spending time with a person when they were around.

Lazy with Cleanliness:
The majority of people do not like to clean. Some though love to clean. Laziness plays a great role with lack of cleanliness. If I am lazy, I will allow things to get messy in my room.

To take an object and return the object to its original place is the golden rule of cleanliness.

Example:
• My laundry is a mountain.

- I throw my socks onto the floor when I get home from work.
- My sink is overflowing with dishes.
- My pantry is empty.
- Trash is full of pizza boxes and instant meals.
- I cannot find my keys.

Laziness starts as a one-time excuse then gradually become a habit difficult to change. Start a routine of "Clean Day" once every couple weeks. Choose a day that works and keep your room/workplace absolutely clean. I need to step out of my comfort zone to let go of laziness.

Beating Laziness:

In order to finish laziness,

- I have to remain enthusiastic. I cheer up myself by keeping the benefits and attainments I will receive in my mind if I do this task/sustain that relationship.
- Determination is another important method. Creating thoughts like "I have to do it no matter what," "Each relationship is important," "I should not waste time but make the best of it" will help. Let us conquer a bit of laziness today.
- To avoid regrets, I need to value the time I have. When I keep this in my awareness, then I conquer laziness. Sometimes it is necessary to care about the consequences of my laziness — What will I lose? What damage will it cause others who depend on me? Will I be able to fix it later?
- With constant awareness and attention, any habit can be reformed. I can take baby steps and devise an action plan to conquer my laziness.

- Lifestyle change is also required in certain cases, e.g., to eat instant food occasionally is all right but to eat them each day is a sign of laziness.

Reflection:
1. What causes laziness for you?
2. Write the effects of your laziness.
3. List some of your laziness habits.
4. Write two of your common excuses.
5. Write the consequences of your laziness that happen to you and others.
6. Devise an action plan to change one habit a month and note down the results.

Om shanti (I am peace)

How to Deal with My Weaknesses

When I am not able to change my weakness/defect;

- If I am in a position of power, I will abuse the power of that position to get away from the consequences of my weak nature, e.g., bossiness
- I will operate in fear of my weakness and force myself to behave so that my weak nature is not expressed, e.g., an office assistant who hides her anger and follows her boss's orders.
- not to use my weak nature with a lot of caution and attention (no fear)
- transform my weak nature into positive with the help of deep reflection, contemplation and meditational practice
- I can use my weakness secretively so that no one knows until watched closer, e.g., greed of personal choices!

These are the three scenarios of people's weaknesses,
- Others are affected by them and I am not, e.g., egoistic
- Only I am affected by them, e.g., grief
- I pay the price of my weakness , e.g., losing a friend due to my habit of doubt.

All of us have one weakness or another. When we express our weaknesses or defects in our actions and relationships, we face retaliation and consequences.

- Most of our defects come out automatically and it is not our intention.
- Intentional and planned.

Whenever someone's weakness is visible in their words and behavior, e.g., jealousy the following category of reactions are observed.

Category 1:
They feel,
- guilty
- sad and dislike themselves
- helpless

Category 2:
They,
- do not realize their defects and they continue with their old patterns
- do not bother to apologize and fix
- are insensitive
- escape

Category 3:
They,
- are intentional and deliberate
- know their weakness and use it to harm others
- consider their weakness to be their power, e.g., the person considers his violence to be his power to control others.

Category 1 people have the habit of apologizing and reconciling while they commit mistakes. At least this shows their pure heart and the empathy they have for others. Even though they are unable to change their weaknesses and defects, they at least try to fix it and make up with others.

Category 2 people do not want to go into that mode. They try to escape from the reality and try to be in denial of the truth. They offer constant justifications of their actions and refuse to change their point of view. They are more on the adamant side and say "I am all fine the way I am and people can put up with me if they want."

Category 3 people are like stone, their heart is fixed and their energy is used in destructive actions. Negativity is their power and they are absolutely happy with it. They identify themselves with their negative qualities and feel justified in their spirit.
No matter what category people are, there are healthy ways to deal with weaknesses.

The Healthy Method to Deal with Weaknesses:
1. Realize
2. Take responsibility
3. Reflect & understand
4. Visualize the change
5. Make baby steps of change
6. Pay attention
7. Reflect and appreciate daily
8. Take power from the Source
9. Patience
10. Final transformation.

It is quite natural to develop low self esteem and become disheartened whenever we are confronted with our weaknesses. Especially when being punished by others for our weak behaviors, but it is essential to start a healthy process of transformation. Not to just sit with the weaknesses and give up on it, or hide it in the cupboard but to bring out and trace the root cause of those negative behaviors.

The above steps explain that the first step is to realize and take responsibility for our actions. To quietly reflect and understand all sides of our personality both positive and negative. Visualize the change of thought, attitude, word and behavior I would like to bring in my life. Take baby steps of those changes and pay attention daily. Appreciate every little improvement and to draw spiritual power from the Source of powers. One more thing, patience is required throughout the process of transformation not haste and expecting quick results. The ground level change takes quality time in reaching the final and permanent transformation of our behavior.

Reflection:
1. Write one or two weaknesses you observe in yourself.
2. Which category of reaction do you fall into during the consequences of your weaknesses?
3. Apply the 10 step transformation process and journal your results.

Om shanti (I am peace)

How to be Free from Desires

Desire means to want something intensely. Desires arise when I am empty within. Desires just temporarily fulfill the emptiness of the being. If I am peace-less, I will desire peace. If I lack love, I will desire love and belongingness. Desires are never-ending, a person with desires can never say all my desires are now finished. Desires make one greedy and discontent. One desire finishes, another starts. It is like a hamster running on a wheel, desires never end. No matter one tries to satisfy the desires, the mind always creates more and something different each time.

When there is complete inner harmony and contentment, no desire arises. When my being is full, there will be no desires. It is like a full pot. When you carry a full pot, there is no noise (no movement of water within the pot). When you carry a half pot, there is always noise (the water shakes and splashes out).

Desire is such a strong desire that one wants to get it no matter what (even if it means you damage others).

Origin of Desires:
1. Comparison — When I start looking at others and see what they have, my desires arise. I want what they have. I feel I also deserve it and create desires — a longing to receive.
2. When I become jealous and envious of others' properties, belongings, talents and facilities then I will create impure

desires to snatch it away from them cunningly or by other means.

3. When I am deprived of what I deserve in my life, I will have desires to own it or experience it.

   Example: I deserve as much love as my sibling brother, but for some reason I did not receive equal love from my parents, then I will always desire that love.

Desires Vs Goals:

Often aims, goals and objectives are confused with desires. Aims and goals have a positive force to achieve something with determination and perseverance. Whereas desires tend to have selfish motives and tend to create harm to others to achieve them.

An ambitious person reaches his goal without hurting others in the process, in fact he/she inspires others and provides opportunities for growth. An ambitious person is always mindful of people's needs around him/her and helps them to grow along with him/her.

A desirous person is blind in achieving his/her desire and do not hesitate to harm others for their own benefit. A desirous person only sees his profit and becomes insensitive to others' needs and problems.

Pure Desires Vs Impure Desires:

Sometimes desires are classified as pure desires where a person wants to fulfill his/her positive desires no matter what. Pure desires are more directed towards the positive beneficial outcome. Still, if pure desires are not fulfilled, one feels bad that's why they are called desires.

When desires are not fulfilled:

- Disheartened and disappointed.
- Low self-esteem — feeling worthless
- Unhappy.
- Longing — When my past desires are not fulfilled, I tend to carry a heavy burden in my heart, e.g., I missed growing up with my father or mother (in case of divorced parents).
- Sometimes even miserable — when many of my desires are not fulfilled, if I am a negative person then I can be even miserable due to it.
- When my desires are not fulfilled even after much hard-work and trials and then when I see a person gets his desires easily fulfilled, I feel injustice, cheated and revengeful.
- I tend to be an obstacle and give a hard time to others. In other words, indirectly I don't want others to be happy. I don't want others to get their desires fulfilled as mine did not.

How to be free from desires:
Meditation:
To make myself full and content, i.e., find a pathway to my inner being to experience inner peace and inner power. This can be done through self-reflection, contemplation, journaling and meditation.

When I start taking from within, I will naturally stop taking from outside.

Shifting from limited to Unlimited:

When I change my attitude from all limited to unlimited, I can easily let go of all temporary worldly desires. Unlimited means the bigger picture and to think beyond the self. To go beyond "I" and "mine." Limited thinking means to only think about my happiness, my family's protection and my growth. To go beyond limited means to allow the inner being to think for the good of the whole world. To see the bigger picture of every situation, to be in tune with the universe's flow of life and to be happy with it. Desires stop when I try not to alter it but move with the flow.

Desires arise when I want something my way. I want it according to my taste, mood, pleasure, person, manner and at a specific moment. When I desire in this way, I am fighting the flow and even disturbing it.

Effort:

Effort is required for success. There is no shortcut or luck for success. Some people believe you need to be lucky to be successful. Spirituality says even luck or good fortune is created through effort.

The right method to receive anything in life is to make the right effort with the right method at the right time and then let it go. The result will find its way to you.

When I believe this law, then there will be no desires to receive something in haste or via force. I do not have to run after things, everything will come to me (The Law of

Attraction). The ability to attract whatever is essential to me comes through pure selfless consciousness.

The heart needs to be clean to attract. The BK teaching says that one who is even beyond the name and trace of desires, is always content and cheerful.

Therefore, I need to make an effort and work towards something I would like to receive or achieve. Offer my best and do hard work, simply to seek is not enough but to work towards the goal will bring success. Effort is always done with determination, patience and perseverance. Effort done with a doubtful intellect and a complaining mind will be futile.

Feel the Abundance and Become Content:
Desires arise when you stop looking at what you have and start looking at what you don't have. When I am able to appreciate all I have received, I will feel content. The feeling of abundance is not external but internal. The more I am able to tune within, the more I can feel the abundant power within me. This connection triggers a feeling of abundance and a deep sense of contentment. When I achieve this state, then desires do not arise and whatever I think, manifests in my life naturally just like magic. This stage is the ultimate stage of spirituality.

Ask any person who is tuned within they will answer they have less desires and their desires do not control them but they manage the desires. Therefore stop tuning out, tune within!

Reflection:
1. Write three desires you have.
2. Write two deep desires that are already fulfilled. How much gratitude and appreciation do you have towards that fulfillment.
3. Out of the three desires, try to change one desire with the above methods and write the results.
4. Try to go a week without any desires and note down the observations.

Om shanti (I am peace)

How to Play Your Inner Music

Everyone loves music. Music moves the heart and holds the power to shift our feelings. There are varieties of music and each of our preferences differ. We tend to lean towards music that carries positive vibes like love songs, meditation music, relaxation music and inspirational songs. That music triggers our inner love, peace, joy and enthusiasm.

There is also music which conveys negative emotions like anger, sadness, hopelessness, frustration and jealousy. We only relate with them because they depict our temporary state of mind at a specific point of our lives. Time to time, we draw from an external source — music to feel better or change our minds. But there is also an inner music in each of us. There is an inner rhythm which we all have and it is unique for each one of us. The rhythm is the way we talk to ourselves. The way to play the music of our soul is silence.

One of the ways to access this inner music is gentle external music. In the extroverted and busy world, we all have forgotten to play our inner music. We all love external music because we were once deeply connected to our inner music. We thought, spoke and acted from the joy of this inner music. The inner music are the tones of knowledge, purity, peace, love, joy, enthusiasm, power and bliss. Then we slowly ignored the inner music and got attracted to the temptations and attractions of the external world.

Example: Being engaged in a video game — the external stimuli keeps you so engaged that you do not have the time and interest to connect within.

Composing your Music:
Check the way you talk to yourself.
• Is it gentle, sweet, loving, encouraging? or
• Is it rude, complaining, blame, guilt, demotivating?
Create your music by knowing yourself and talk to yourself in the way you talk to your friend/child/loved one. The inner music is your sweet energizing conversation with yourself. Below are some of the approaches you can try.
• Acknowledge your actions.
• Appreciate your good thoughts, words and behavior.
• Rewind and Replay positive memories in your mind. Recollect inspirational positive points of wisdom.
• Remember God, His presence, His love and your connection with Him.

Below are some varieties of inner music.
Melody of love and sweetness: Sing songs of your specialties, strengths, virtues and powers. As you sing, you can also do a tap dance.

Folk Music of Respect and Dignity: The idea of self-respect is to build your self-esteem, not feed your ego. The manner to address yourself is to cultivate self-worth without losing the ground of humility. You understand that everyone deserves respect and one cannot disrespect the other due to their lack of talent, capacity and material wealth. The respect we cultivate in this rhythm is non-materialistic and applied towards the inner beauty of each soul.

Wrong Music:
When you,
- criticize yourself
- blame yourself
- defame yourself
- dislike yourself

That is like playing the wrong beat that will only make you experience anger, hatred and unhappiness. By repeatedly playing this kind of music, you become demoralized.

Punk Rock:
When you,
- bully
- judge
- hate
- criticize
- blame
- hurt

others
When you play these thoughts and feelings in your mind, it is as if you are playing the punk music. All the rhythm of waste and negative thoughts only rob you and others of inner peace.

Broken Record:
When you fall into a deep dark pit of loneliness and low self-worth, you experience depression. It is like a broken record, even though you want to restart your inner music, you are

unable to play it. You need an external jumpstart to glue your broken record.

Spend Time with the Maestro:
Whenever your inner rhythm is not good, just sit with the maestro (God/the Source) and start composing new music of acceptance, tolerance, patience, sweetness and compassion along with Him. Take guidance and support from your maestro. Learn and follow His steps.
When I am able to master this art of inner music and become an excellent music director, then I will be in complete alignment of my inner world and harmonize with everything external. Let us start playing our inner music as well as admire the music of our fellow souls.

Reflection:
1. What types of inner music do you compose?
2. Identify your punk music and edit it.
3. Note down a beautiful inner music composed by your friend and appreciate it, maybe even make it your own.

Om Shanti (I am peace)

About the Author

Padmapriya Mahendarkar Alias Sister Priya is the Meditation Center Coordinator of the Brahma Kumaris, St. Louis branch and a Raja Yoga meditation practitioner since 2002.

She has Bachelors in Information Science and Masters of Business Administration and has worked in the Telecom industry at India for eight years. At 2009, she dedicated her life with the Brahma Kumaris and became a full-fledged Raja Yoga teacher in USA.

Since then she has been facilitating self-development classes and workshops for people from all walks of life. Her classes are simple, engaging and motivational. Her guided meditation commentaries are soothing and provides deep experiences to the listener.

Sister Priya is the author of "100 Inspirational Thoughts Part 1," "The Incredible Power Within," and "Harmony in Relationships" books. For any questions on the book, feel free to email at bksisterpriya@gmail.com

About the Brahma Kumaris

The Brahma Kumaris World Spiritual Organization acknowledges the intrinsic goodness of all people. They teach a practical method of meditation that helps individuals understand their inner strengths and values.

A worldwide family of individuals from all walks of life, they are committed to spiritual growth and personal transformation, believing it to be essential in creating a peaceful and just world.

The Brahma Kumaris World Spiritual University in Mt. Abu, India, is an international non–governmental organization (NGO) in general consultative status with the Economic and Social Council of the United Nations and in consultative status with UNICEF. It is also affiliated to the UN Department of Public Information.

Through its international network of centers, the BK's organize special activities, seminars, workshops, dialogues, conferences, and exhibitions to provide people with spaces to voice their opinions on critical matters that impact their daily lives.

Raja Yoga Meditation

The Raja Yoga Meditation taught by the Brahma Kumaris comprises the three following segments;

Relationship with the Self:
This session provides the BK Teachings on knowing the self, understanding and embracing the strengths and weaknesses of the self. To discover the inner beauty and experience the original virtues of the self. Once the self is understood it paves the way to easy transformation of negative into positive. This session also helps one to understand one's thought patterns, habits and nature.

Relationship with the Source:
This session provides the BK teachings on One Source, the ability and process to tap into the Universal Source of powers. To connect with God without religion but with a direct loving relationship. To experience the spiritual connection between the self and God and recharge the inner self.

Relationship with Karma:
This session provides the BK Teachings on the importance of time and actions. To understand the effect of every action in this world and how to align our thoughts, words and actions. To learn the deep philosophy of Karma and cultivate a natural

way of giving happiness and taking happiness in our relationships.

To learn meditation:

To find your local BK center, go to www.us.brahmakumaris.org and look under "Locations."

Made in the USA
Columbia, SC
25 June 2021